100 Top Tips for Writers:

"Keep Writing!" ~ Viki
By Viki Winterton

20-Time #1 International Best-Selling Author
and Award-Winning Publisher

101 Top Tips for Writers: "Keep Writing!" ~ Viki
By Viki Winterton

Expert Insights Publishing
8640 University City Blvd., Suite A-3 #247
Charlotte, NC 28213

ISBN-13: 978-1546882237
ISBN-10: 1546882235

Cover Design: Terry Z
Edited by: Pam Murphy

15 14 13 12 11 1 2 3 4 5

A portion of the profits from this book will be donated to Proliteracy Worldwide, Championing the power of literacy to improve the lives of adults and their families, communities, and societies

Dedication

To all writers:

"Get your story out across the globe.
Your story untold is forever lost.
Your story untold leaves a hole in the world,
No one can tell your unique story.
Only you can do this.
Your story is your gift to the world.
Telling your story to the world is your responsibility.
Keep writing."

~ Viki

Table of Contents

Discover the mindset tips to make writing easy!

Use this proven formula to make your writing
irresistible to your readers!

Clarify the purpose of your writing to strengthen your
message!

Craft a message that will inform minds and capture
hearts from cover to cover!

Introduction

Welcome to *100 Top Tips For Writers*. This interactive little book shares some often overlooked, powerful tips, above and beyond writing technique. I have personally used these to author 20 #1 International bestsellers and promote over 1,000 additional authors to bestseller status. You are encouraged at each tip to capture your creative thoughts as you share your story with the world.

Everything you discover will enable you to stand out from the noise and have your potential readers be naturally drawn to you.

Books change lives every moment. A book is unique, unlike any other media. Many people try to write a book but only a few succeed. If you have completed your book, you are part of a small, exclusive group of people in this world.

Authoring a book enables you to spread your message and broaden your horizons beyond your wildest dreams. Your book is the end of one period of work, and the beginning of a more important one. In your book, you can lay the groundwork for your whole life's platform to success. It is not your final word; it's only the start of your conversation.

Your book is your most widely accepted credential in the largest number of venues. Your book is often your most attractive asset to TV studios, radio shows, speaking events, boardrooms, web pages, newsprint and, most importantly, people's minds. This book will show you why it is critical to think of your book as a tool that will benefit other people while expanding your business and your platform.

Make your book a realization of your dreams as you think of ways to send your message to your chosen audience. Make your book worthwhile to read, engaging, and with a call to action. Look beyond publishing and selling to the many creative ways you and the world can prosper from your book.

Your book shouldn't contain all you know. It should be an enticing entry to your world and your current and future assets – your other work and writings, videos, trainings, events, products, speeches, teachings, broadcast, web presence and affiliations – as your world continues to expand over time.

Getting published and having your book out in the world is not the end of the journey. It is the start for you to build your platform, your name and expertise. Tap into this perfect tool to breathe life into your platform and your reputation as THE EXPERT in your field.

Chapter 1 -
It's All About You

Discover the mindset tips to make writing easy!

"There is no greater agony than bearing an untold story inside you."
— Maya Angelou

Have you ever felt a certain hesitation when you're about to start a new project? You may have had doubts on your ability to fulfill it, or fears of being met by criticism. These are natural feelings, especially when the project you're going to work on is something of huge significance to you.

Writing a book is just such a project. You may be able to pour your heart and soul into writing a masterpiece, but there's still the matter of whether it will bring you the rewards you seek. Even seasoned authors can't help but ask themselves this question before writing a new book: Will it help me reach my goals?

Thankfully, it takes only a little creativity and resourcefulness to ease your worries. Even better, you can start making financial headway right at the very beginning – even before you write the book itself, before you write a word!

Now, discover these top writers' tips, capture your creative thoughts and share your unique story with the world!

Tip 1: "Writer's block starts with the Mindset."

Saying that you have writer's block, often starts the process very effectively. Remember that your story, the one you are writing, has a beginning and an end. Knowing your message will be heard, writer's block can end by not uttering these first two words. What can you do to propel your creativity?

_____
_____
_____
_____
_____
_____
_____
_____
_____
_____
_____
_____
_____
_____
_____
_____
_____

Tip 2: "Every story has a story."

Inside of every story, there are layers of other stories. Each time you write on one topic, stop and reflect on deeper topics that support your story. Knowing this tip will help you write stronger with every idea. Has your big idea come forth? What are some layers of stories that can support it?

_____

_____

_____

_____

_____

_____

_____

_____

_____

_____

_____

_____

_____

_____

_____

_____

_____

_____

Tip 3: "Write as you would read."

While you may be inclined to write as others would read, sometimes it's a promising idea to write as you would read. What are some of the sentences or underlying messages you like to enjoy? These are good places to expand your writing skills.

_____

_____

_____

_____

_____

_____

_____

_____

_____

_____

_____

_____

_____

_____

_____

_____

_____

_____

_____

Tip 4: "Stay focused on results."

The greatest way to succeed as a writer or author is to focus on the intended results of your writing. Name them and work on perfecting the words you use to describe each result. Do you want to "excite your reader"? Then think about the excitement on their face when flipping through your book.

_____

_____

_____

_____

_____

_____

_____

_____

_____

_____

_____

_____

_____

_____

_____

_____

_____

_____

Tip 5: "Stop if you feel sleepy."

If you feel like you are going to fall asleep, stop and get some water. Face-planting onto your laptop is never a clever idea. You also won't write your best if you are exhausted. Even if you are tempted to write sleepy, try to wake up a little for your most powerful message. What renews your energy and fuels your heart, mind and spirit?

_____

_____

_____

_____

_____

_____

_____

_____

_____

_____

_____

_____

_____

_____

_____

_____

_____

_____

Tip 6: "Words are like music; allow them to flow."

The most magical aspect of any written piece is the ease by which words flow into the mind. When writing for expression, feel the flow of energy through your soul, out your fingertips and into the heart of your reader. How do you get into the flow?

_____

_____

_____

_____

_____

_____

_____

_____

_____

_____

_____

_____

_____

_____

_____

_____

_____

_____

_____

Tip 7: "See your book 30 years from today, in the hands of someone you are helping."

Looking at your book through the lens of the future allows you to move into a place in your mind, where success has already happened and continues happening through time and space. You will see those books that have sustained, have had layers of success and are timeless in their impact. What legacy would you like to leave through your book?

_____
_____
_____
_____
_____
_____
_____
_____
_____
_____
_____
_____
_____
_____
_____
_____

Tip 8: "Even if it's all about you, refrain from starting every sentence with the word "I."

One of the great tragedies of writing as an art form is in using the word "I" at the beginning of every sentence. A good tip is to challenge yourself to start each paragraph with a unique word containing different letters of the alphabet.

_____
_____
_____
_____
_____
_____
_____
_____
_____
_____
_____
_____
_____
_____
_____
_____
_____
_____
_____

Tip 9: "See a big book inside of you, rather than a spineless book that is written swiftly."

Sure, anyone can write a book, but do you enjoy holding a 40-page book in your hand? This is a great tip for you if you feel like you want to quit. Take your time and allow your book to build to 150-200 pages for maximum reader impact. When tempted to quit, what keeps you going?

_____

_____

_____

_____

_____

_____

_____

_____

_____

_____

_____

_____

_____

_____

_____

_____

_____

_____

Tip 10: "Complete your front book cover."

Promote your "soon-to-be-released" book with your front book cover. All it needs is a little tweak on your existing and new promotional tools, internet posts, media releases, business cards, email signature and more to highlight your big book project. How can you get others involved in your project before you even write a word?

_____

_____

_____

_____

_____

_____

_____

_____

_____

_____

_____

_____

_____

_____

_____

_____

Chapter 2 -
It's All About Your Audience
Use this proven formula to make your writing
irresistible to your readers!

"Write the kind of story you would like to read. People will give you all sorts of advice about writing, but if you are not writing something you like, no one else will like it either."
— Meg Cabot

Are you all set to write your remarkable masterpiece? It is ideal to find your book buyers' profile first, figure out what they are eager to learn and read, research to see if it is unique, and then start writing.

Select your target audience and deliver your best to them.

Develop your Table of Contents first on the topics that you want to include in your book. This will make it easier for you to compose your thoughts and be coherent with your ideas. Some books that have been published out there successfully gave headaches to readers. The reason behind this – there was no clarity or relationship to the title and its poorly written content!

Your well written book is a gift to your readers and a responsibility for you.

Now, discover these top writers' tips, capture your creative thoughts and share your unique story with the world!

Tip 11: "Allow emotions to reveal themselves TOO without hiding your brilliance."

Your story has high impact. Even those times when you stomped your foot and shot out those vulgar words count as emotions that your readers want to experience. Let them LOL and ROFL with you. Think of an experience you could share.

_____

_____

_____

_____

_____

_____

_____

_____

_____

_____

_____

_____

_____

_____

_____

_____

_____

_____

_____

Tip 12: "Thirteen is not a bad number and a great total number of sections and chapters to have in your book."

This tip is for the building of your book structure. When you have a terrific book idea, having 3 sections with 4 chapters each, and an additional chapter to grow on, your book is balanced. Balance is key is formatting and structuring your masterpiece. Can you identify 3 sections and 4 chapter titles for your book?

_____

_____

_____

_____

_____

_____

_____

_____

_____

_____

_____

_____

_____

_____

Tip 13: "Notebooks are the New Black."

Don't get tied down to the notion that you must be on your computer to write a book because the inspiration comes at all times of the day and night. Even on Christmas morning or while changing a flat tire on a dreadful day, ideas come to you that deserve to be captured. Keep a notebook with you everywhere. Capture some creative thoughts now.

_____

_____

_____

_____

_____

_____

_____

_____

_____

_____

_____

_____

_____

_____

_____

_____

Tip 14: "Grab your spouse and read out loud to them."

Reading out loud what you write on paper helps you to add energy and impact to your words. Watch your partner's facial expression for signs of hypnosis; this is where the magic resides. Your words should penetrate the mind and play with the soul. Make a reading date.

_____
_____
_____
_____
_____
_____
_____
_____
_____
_____
_____
_____
_____
_____
_____
_____
_____
_____
_____

Tip 15: "Don't stop short of Gold: Keep Going Always."

Writing a book drains you and fulfills you at the same time. As you are going through the other tips and tricks be sure to evaluate where you are as you are trying to find a stopping point. You may go back and read something that needs changing and feel discouraged. Feel the fear and write anyway. What inspiring quote or saying keeps you going?

_____

_____

_____

_____

_____

_____

_____

_____

_____

_____

_____

_____

_____

_____

_____

_____

_____

Tip 16: "Blogging can become your book if you are consistent with your message."

One of the easiest tips I have for you is that to become a published author with a decent sized book, is to intend that your blog will be your book. Categorizing your blog topics can actually serve as chapters in your big, bountiful book. What is an ideal blog topic for your book?

_____

_____

_____

_____

_____

_____

_____

_____

_____

_____

_____

_____

_____

_____

_____

_____

_____

_____

Tip 17: "Social media teaches you the art of short writing."

One of the most profound changes in recent times is the dawn of short language. Incorporating practice in short writing will help you add flow and flavor to your book or writing project. Although not fully accepted and literarily correct, using language that appeals to Millennials and younger, helps add depth to your creativity.

Tip 18: "Using a Word Processor for valuable ideas."

Microsoft Word has added tons of features for writers including suggested replacements for familiar words. This will show up to you as a dotted line under a series of words. When you right click on the set of words, suggestions pop up like magic. Try it!

_____
_____
_____
_____
_____
_____
_____
_____
_____
_____
_____
_____
_____
_____
_____
_____
_____

Tip 19: "Write your Character Sheet first in a Novel."

When you have a novel living in you like JK Rowling did with *Harry Potter*, the actors in the theatre of your imagination start to take shape. Rather than jumping into writing the story, take some time and develop your characters deeply. Before you even start writing, get so close to your characters that you know their birthdays as well as your own child.

Tip 20: "Don't write to please the World."

Perhaps the greatest tragedy is in writing to please others first, without first pleasing yourself. Remember that you want to love your book and it wants to give you love in return. Whether you are writing for yourself or others, find the sweet spots that appeal to your audience.

Chapter 3 -
It's All About Your Vision

Clarify the purpose of your writing to
strengthen your message!

"You can't wait for inspiration.
You have to go after it with a club."
— Jack London

Discovering your book's purpose comes down to two basic things:

* Know yourself deeply
* Know what you want

The more you know yourself, the more you are able to articulate what you want to communicate in your book and in your life. From that will come discovering your purpose.

Listen. Listen to your own self. Quiet time allows you to hear your inner voice.

Stay Aware. Staying in present time allows you to notice in more detail what you are experiencing as you move through life, what you are experiencing from moment to moment.

Focus. If you can focus on your intention, listen, and remain aware, you may be surprised at how many choices open up as you move down the path of your purpose and passion with your vision guiding you.

Now, discover these top writers' tips, capture your creative thoughts and share your unique story with the world!

Tip 21: "Emotions Drive Action. Use them powerfully."

Knowing when to add emotions and emotional topics requires you to feel out the emotions, which may cause a reaction or call to action. When you want to write about happiness, use adverbs, adjectives and exclamation points to show your level of emotion. If you are writing about pain, you can call out your reader with "Do you know what I mean?", thus attaching to their emotion and inviting them to act.

Tip 22: "Transition Lightly with the ..."

The triple dots you use all of the time, actually mean a 360 in thought process. You are writing to convey a message and changing your thoughts every 2.1 seconds is not an effective way to draw and keep attention. Be sure to use this grammar switch sparingly. What is an example of powerful usage?

_____

_____

_____

_____

_____

_____

_____

_____

_____

_____

_____

_____

_____

_____

_____

_____

_____

_____

Tip 23: "Start with 10."

To write a 150-page book, create an outline that allows for 10 chapters with 10 pages each and 50 pages to play with. Ten pages is not a lot to write and a good outline will help you get there faster. For each chapter, plan on at least 10 pages. Ten pages is about 10,000 words – maybe a little more. Don't be intimidated by the number of words because the words will flow like water when your vision guides you to write.

Tip 24: "Go deeper with your top-level Topics."

You will come up with 10 categories pretty quickly, but go one step further and have your category to include 5 bullet points of potential sub-topics. For example, if you are using the Law of Attraction as your top-level topic, try using (1) Attracting Money (2) Changing your Tone ... these are some ideas for writing prompts using sub-topics. Sub-topics should define the benefits of reading your book for your audience. List some of your book's benefits to readers.

_____

_____

_____

_____

_____

_____

_____

_____

_____

_____

_____

_____

_____

_____

_____

_____

_____

Tip 25: "Take time to write for Fun."

Sometimes it is an awesome idea to just write for fun, in a whimsical manner, just for the love of doing it. The greatest authors in the world have taken time to have fun writing. Try writing a pretend comic strip, or a broad vision of what you would like to create in your life.

_____

_____

_____

_____

_____

_____

_____

_____

_____

_____

_____

_____

_____

_____

_____

_____

_____

_____

_____

Tip 26: "Protect your words with Trademarks."

When you write paragraphs and short posts for social media, the quotes you make could be quotes of a lifetime. When you coin a phrase, or saying, add the ™ to it and consider getting a legal trademark on your quote. You never know when someone may want to use your words supplied by your vision.

_____
_____
_____
_____
_____
_____
_____
_____
_____
_____
_____
_____
_____
_____
_____
_____
_____
_____

Tip 27: "Go back to the big dictionary."

Online media has made it easier than ever before to go to Google for all of life's many answers, but there are words you may not know exist, which can help you add depth and vibrancy to your writing. Take some time and find 5 words per week in the Dictionary and incorporate those into your writing.

_____

_____

_____

_____

_____

_____

_____

_____

_____

_____

_____

_____

_____

_____

_____

_____

_____

_____

_____

_____

Tip 28: "Stay focused and stop when needed."

If you are like most authors, you begin writing and then veer off into worlds unknown. Stay focused on your writing paragraph by paragraph, stopping as needed to read, reflect and restart. Doing this will help you keep your message clear.

_____

_____

_____

_____

_____

_____

_____

_____

_____

_____

_____

_____

_____

_____

_____

_____

_____

_____

_____

Tip 29: "Follow the Leaders."

Keep your favorite books around you so you can mimic the styles of those you enjoy the most. If you love a great romantic novel, and are interested in self-help books, both of these provide great insight into writing forms that stick in the mind. If you love a book, then writing in that style will engage a wide array of readers.

Tip 30: "Stop worrying about being a good writer."

The idea is to write the vision inside of you. Worrying about perfectionism will only hinder you and your writing will never be born to the world. Track down good books of old and see how "imperfect" the author's writing was compared to the requirements today.

_____

_____

_____

_____

_____

_____

_____

_____

_____

_____

_____

_____

_____

_____

_____

_____

_____

_____

Chapter 4 -
It's All About Your Magical Message
Craft a message that will inform minds and
capture hearts from cover to cover!

"Tears are words that need to be written."
— Paulo Coelho

Craft your individual message and use it to reach out to others, change lives, and captivate hearts. Each of us has a unique message to share with the world.

To write a good book you must be inspired. Dig deep to share your most authentic thoughts.

Wherever you are right now is the perfect place to start moving toward the goal of writing your book so that others can begin to be moved by your message.

Identify the message you would like to share based on your target audience's interests, needs and desires.

You may what want to start with a shorter book so the task does not seem so daunting.

Embark on a journey that will help you find your gift, explore your talents, and teach you to touch lives with your passion, purpose and story. Discover what it takes to make your message magical.

Now, discover these top writers' tips, capture your creative thoughts and share your unique story with the world!

Tip 31: "Writing in longhand before you type adds flavor."

Re-ignite the flame of writing with a pen on a notebook as you are having brilliant ideas. Get inspired. Take time to go outdoors and allow the inspiration of nature to be part of your journey in writing.

_____

_____

_____

_____

_____

_____

_____

_____

_____

_____

_____

_____

_____

_____

_____

_____

_____

Tip 32: "Visit the bookstore often and pay attention."

Have you ever gone to your local book store and just allowed your fingers to flow over the books on the shelves? If so, then you probably noticed some books that stand out and others that don't. Pay attention to the ones that call to you and pick up that book. What's inside? Is it the cover graphic?

_____

_____

_____

_____

_____

_____

_____

_____

_____

_____

_____

_____

_____

_____

_____

_____

_____

_____

Tip 33: "Take advantage of online writing opportunities."

Everyone could use some exposure when writing. There are many outlets on the Internet where writers can be seen and add their articles. One is Ezinearticles.com. This is a great place to start seeing your writing come to life. Plan some submissions.

_____

_____

_____

_____

_____

_____

_____

_____

_____

_____

_____

_____

_____

_____

_____

_____

_____

_____

Tip 34: "Read more books."

As simple as this sounds, the more you read, the better you write. Seeing how successful books formulate paragraphs, text indents, call-out blocks and sentence structure, helps you fashion your successful writing plan. What are your favorites?

_____

_____

_____

_____

_____

_____

_____

_____

_____

_____

_____

_____

_____

_____

_____

_____

_____

_____

Tip 35: "Write from the Heart."

When writing your autobiography, remember you are memorializing your life so your legacy can be realized. Be sure to write those times that made you smile, took your breath away, or made you sad. Leave your legacy as you know it, not as someone may interpret it after you are gone.

_____

_____

_____

_____

_____

_____

_____

_____

_____

_____

_____

_____

_____

_____

_____

_____

_____

_____

Tip 36: "Remembering the Good Times."

As you are telling your story in any written work, remember the good times. In life, sharing your joy helps others experience joy in their own life. The funniest things in your memory bank are worthy of being read by someone else.

_____

_____

_____

_____

_____

_____

_____

_____

_____

_____

_____

_____

_____

_____

_____

_____

_____

_____

_____

_____

Tip 37: "Write about Sad Times."

Just like writing your joy, writing your tears is important. You can do this. Writing about the sad times invokes the tip on healing. Sadness is just an emotion that works alongside happiness, fear and disgust. When you are feeling sad, you don't want to stay that way. Writing about how you moved from sad to glad is a good way to help your readers.

_____

_____

_____

_____

_____

_____

_____

_____

_____

_____

_____

_____

_____

_____

_____

_____

Tip 38: "Research Culture Language."

A Cajun has a different dialect, much different than a Canadian ehe? Understanding language that has a cultural twist can help add flavor to your writing. Australians and British say "mum" rather than "mom". Have a conversation with someone who is from another country, a distant land and just listen.

Tip 39: "Write Unique word with Every Letter."

Try your hand and word Wizardry and get a sheet of paper. Write one word for every letter of the alphabet and then a sentence. Get into your dictionary and choose words you have never used before. Then, use these words in your writing. Pretty soon you will have a whole notebook filled.

Tip 40: "Engage the senses."

There is nothing better than imagining the aroma of bacon cooking on the stove, when reading a book or story. Engaging the senses is a wonderful way to really allow your reader to fully be present in your writing. What does the reader see, smell, feel or hear in your writing?

_____
_____
_____
_____
_____
_____
_____
_____
_____
_____
_____
_____
_____
_____
_____
_____
_____
_____

Tip 41: "Play with the Action Tense."

When you are writing, and want your reader to really feel out your words, change up the "Action Tense" and see how that works. Instead of saying "I went to the house", say "Upon Arriving at the House". This is a fun way to incorporate unique twists into your writing.

_____
_____
_____
_____
_____
_____
_____
_____
_____
_____
_____
_____
_____
_____
_____
_____
_____
_____

Tip 42: "Avoid Wordiness."

This can be very hard to do, especially when you are trying very hard to write your very best story in the shortest amount of time and you are wanting to get more words in that impact so you continue to write with more words than are needed to express your opinion or thought in the project you are writing with. (Get the Picture?).

_____

_____

_____

_____

_____

_____

_____

_____

_____

_____

_____

_____

_____

_____

_____

_____

_____

_____

Tip 43: "Write about Every Holiday."

Memories are made at the holidays and every holiday that you celebrate in your own soul circle, has a priceless piece of inspiration. Writing about the holidays can give you more ideas for future writing. The food has its own story as do the people. Families connect, bond and often separate and fight during the holidays. Capture some memories here.

_____
_____
_____
_____
_____
_____
_____
_____
_____
_____
_____
_____
_____
_____
_____
_____
_____
_____

Tip 44: "Take ideas from all around you and look at opportunities to create stories, book chapters or lessons."

Inside Out is a children's movie that features the subconscious mind of a child and the characters are emotions such as anger, fear and sadness. This movie provides great insights on how emotions can be personified. This is a simple tip to spark your creative imagination.

_____
_____
_____
_____
_____
_____
_____
_____
_____
_____
_____
_____
_____
_____
_____
_____
_____
_____

Tip 45: "Keep a Journal."

Keeping a journal of your feelings can help you see the ups and downs you took, as an author, while giving birth to your book or writing. Journal every emotion you have, every idea you entertain and every doubt that pops into your mind.

_____
_____
_____
_____
_____
_____
_____
_____
_____
_____
_____
_____
_____
_____
_____
_____
_____
_____
_____
_____

Tip 46: "Get a new laptop."

If you are running an old laptop, with outdated software, you are not doing yourself a favor as a writer. Just go out and spend the money. Buy a new laptop and reap the rewards.

_____
_____
_____
_____
_____
_____
_____
_____
_____
_____
_____
_____
_____
_____
_____
_____
_____
_____
_____
_____
_____

Tip 47: "Do Your Best."

Even if you quit school in the 5th grade, do your best. Practice writing. Practice reading. Write and then read. You can do the best you can do every moment that you are willing to keep trying. Writing is never going away, so just do it.

_____
_____
_____
_____
_____
_____
_____
_____
_____
_____
_____
_____
_____
_____
_____
_____
_____
_____
_____
_____

Tip 48: "Eradicate Self-Doubt."

The one major emotion that stops writers from succeeding is in doubting that they are good writers. You are a great writer. Your story is important. Try very hard to eradicate self-doubt by using intentional affirmations that counterbalance doubt. Say affirmations such as "I write really well".

_____
_____
_____
_____
_____
_____
_____
_____
_____
_____
_____
_____
_____
_____
_____
_____
_____
_____

Tip 49: "Map Your Life."

You can create your own life map in writing and it's a great way to leave reminders to your children of where you came from. Adding personalized lessons such as "Who am I?" can help you expand your writing into real life situations that happened to you on the journey.

_____

_____

_____

_____

_____

_____

_____

_____

_____

_____

_____

_____

_____

_____

_____

_____

_____

_____

Tip 50: "Be the Change."

As you are writing for others, you can start to be the change. This means that you can actually morph your real life into something that you are dreaming of in your writing. If you are writing about a super hero, then by all means, get out your cape.

_____

_____

_____

_____

_____

_____

_____

_____

_____

_____

_____

_____

_____

_____

_____

_____

_____

_____

_____

_____

_____

Tip 51: "POV and understanding the difference."

Point of view means the "person" (as in 1st, 2nd, or 3rd, and not the character's voice) the writer uses when telling the story. However, when people talk about POV, they sometimes refer to the character who is telling the story. Write in a consistent voice.

_____

_____

_____

_____

_____

_____

_____

_____

_____

_____

_____

_____

_____

_____

_____

_____

_____

_____

_____

_____

Tip 52: "Outlining a novel."

Novels are not like self-help books. They must go deeply into the mind of the reader to create an addiction. Much like the book series *Harry Potter*, your books must compel in order to convert to a best-selling series. This tip helps you set the scene for your exciting novel. Write a list of everything you already know about your story. You'll probably come to this step with a handful of scenes already in mind. Even if you have no idea how these scenes will play out in the story, go ahead and add them to the list.

_____

_____

_____

_____

_____

_____

_____

_____

_____

_____

_____

_____

_____

_____

Tip 53: "Explore Online Learning Opportunities."

Ezine Articles is a great resource for you to practice writing. Not only does the approval team point out grammar errors, but they make suggestions for changes. Often the greatest writer's block is in the fear of missing grammar situations. By participating in opportunities to have your writing published, you start the process of becoming a writer.

Tip 54: "Start where you Stop."

If you finish one book, start the next one from where you stopped the last one. Keeping 5 or 6 book ideas running in your mind at all times, means you will keep publishing books or writing articles that focus on a continuing topic.

Chapter 5 -
It's All About Your Value

Establish your position as THE expert in your field.

"History will be kind to me for I intend to write it."
— Winston S. Churchill

Are you the best kept secret in your field?

Writing as a passion is a wonderful gift. It draws people to respect you and consider you as an expert in your chosen field.

You can gain massive recognition and create a rock-solid reputation as a renowned leader through your book.

Your book allows you to expand your presence, extend your influence and enhance your vision so you can present the world your unique gifts and offerings.

If you yearn to reach out and create positive transformations for as many people as you can, start writing.

Share your vision, imagination, positive thoughts, great advice and ideas across the globe by sharing your story in your book.

Now, discover these top writers' tips, capture your creative thoughts and share your unique story with the world!

Tip 55: "The difference between being a writer and an author."

You may be an author with an amazing book idea, but not be a writer. Sometimes a good tip is to outsource a ghostwriter to assist you in completing you book. When you are a writer, you write for all types of reasons from writing in a newspaper or magazine, to going full out and ghostwriting a book.

Tip 56: "Writing Powerful Social Media Posts."

Let's face it; social media (aka Facebook, Twitter and LinkedIn) requires you to write succinctly and powerfully from the start. Because your words are limited, social media posts will require you to have muscle with words. Take some time and see what posts stand out for you, then create your own.

_____

_____

_____

_____

_____

_____

_____

_____

_____

_____

_____

_____

_____

_____

_____

_____

_____

_____

_____

_____

_____

Tip 57: "Protect your eyesight."

One of the most ignored warnings is on Q-Tips that says "Do not use this in your ear canal". Why do you think that this is the most ignored warning? Because 99% of the people who buy Q-Tips stick them in their ear! When you are writing a lot, don't let this warning slip by you: Gamma Rays from a computer screen are harmful to your eyes. Take time to write your stories and books in a notebook then dedicate certain hours to computer time. Keep your screen dimmed just a little so that the light won't impact you as much.

_____
_____
_____
_____
_____
_____
_____
_____
_____
_____
_____
_____
_____

Tip 58: "Be observant."

Being aware of the things around you helps you to be a better writer. Knowing the new topics that are hot off the press, the new language of readers, as well as future events in your local area helps you write with power and poise.

Tip 59: "Ditch those who don't support you."

One thing a writer must protect is his or her sanity at all times. As you become famous as an author, you may collect critical people who do their best to drag you down. Ditch them and move forward, pride intact, into the success you desire.

_____

_____

_____

_____

_____

_____

_____

_____

_____

_____

_____

_____

_____

_____

_____

_____

_____

_____

Tip 60: "The Power of IDEA."

One of the greatest realizations that comes from writing is the appearance of more and more ideas in your soul. The power of IDEA is within you. Pay attention to hints from your soul, when you are writing and an idea pops in your head.

_____

_____

_____

_____

_____

_____

_____

_____

_____

_____

_____

_____

_____

_____

_____

_____

_____

_____

_____

_____

_____

Tip 61: "Change up your words."

A Dictionary and Thesaurus are valuable tools for writing with words that flow and grow. Simple words can expand, and expanded words can be simplified. Mix it up.

_____

_____

_____

_____

_____

_____

_____

_____

_____

_____

_____

_____

_____

_____

_____

_____

_____

_____

_____

_____

Tip 62: "Enter your writing in contests."

There are thousands of contests that go on daily around the world for writers who can create impactful work. Try your hand at one or more writing contests. This is a wonderful way to get visibility.

_____

_____

_____

_____

_____

_____

_____

_____

_____

_____

_____

_____

_____

_____

_____

_____

_____

_____

_____

_____

_____

Tip 63: "Learn grammar rules and how to break them."

While this may sound counter-intuitive, grammar is fluid. Grammar rules have been around since the dawn of humanity, and breaking them can be done with effect and impact. Know when to use a comma and when to talk the short code LOL.

Tip 64: "Shadow the experts."

When you want to be a published author, you must know what authors you love. Pay attention to every detail of how they do things and imagine that your platform or book success matches theirs.

_____

_____

_____

_____

_____

_____

_____

_____

_____

_____

_____

_____

_____

_____

_____

_____

_____

_____

_____

_____

Chapter 6 -
It's All About Your Brand

Spin the magic of your message
to define your brand

"Description begins in the writer's imagination, but should finish in the reader's."
— Stephen King

Your image is what the reader sees, hears or feels. When what the reader sees, hears and feels all match up with your brand, this builds a sense of trust and loyalty. People feel comfortable and confident that you are who you say you are and that you can deliver what they need. When your book brand is consistent with your business brand, it will turn readers into clients because they trust you! It is easy for them to say "yes."

Design elements, which attract and engage your ideal readers and clients, that radiate the spirit of your work are key factors in building a strong brand. This influences both how much success you will enjoy and how much ease and flow you will experience.

This is good news! Choosing how you, your book and your business are represented visually empowers you to attract positive and rewarding experiences. Building a strong brand will skyrocket your success.

Now, discover these top writers' tips, capture your creative thoughts and share your unique story with the world!

Tip 65: "Less is more in a book cover."

When you are putting together your book cover, remember that less is more. While you may be extremely tempted to add tons of color, flashes of light, polka-dotted unicorns or shiny stars, on the shelf or online, less is more. Remember, your "soon-to-be-released" book front cover is the most powerful preview of your story and reinforces your brand.

_____

_____

_____

_____

_____

_____

_____

_____

_____

_____

_____

_____

_____

_____

_____

_____

_____

_____

Tip 66: "Share often."

Share your work often. On every change you make, let people know about your book's progress. Even if you just have an idea for a book, go tell someone and give that book life. Let your book be born.

_____
_____
_____
_____
_____
_____
_____
_____
_____
_____
_____
_____
_____
_____
_____
_____
_____
_____
_____
_____

Tip 67: "Hire a Proof Reader."

You can read and re-read your work a million times in your voice, but may miss very critical pieces and consistency of your brand. It's often good to retain someone to read your work for you. Maybe even ask a family member to read your writing for you and offer their honest critique.

Tip 68: "Read Out Loud to a Friend."

Plan a book reading party with your friends. Take them out to a nice dinner and read from your book. Observe their emotions and how they react to your content. Is your book representing you and your brand? Make any changes that need to be made based on what they share with you. This is a fun way to find out if you write with as much power as you speak.

_____

_____

_____

_____

_____

_____

_____

_____

_____

_____

_____

_____

_____

_____

_____

_____

_____

Tip 69: "Your story and brand can shine in a book anthology."

Writing with a team is fun and rewarding. Many anthologies have book signing parties and support each other online. Being part of an anthology allows you to write a single chapter in a book featuring many writers who write about a specific topic.

_____
_____
_____
_____
_____
_____
_____
_____
_____
_____
_____
_____
_____
_____
_____
_____
_____
_____
_____
_____

Tip 70: "Consider expressing your brand in an audio book."

Your audience may need more from you than just words on paper. Audio books are a fun addition to your book. You can have a whole book in audio format or have parts of your book narrated by someone. Find a narrator that has the voice fitting to your book. Try out some audiobooks for yourself and test them out.

_____
_____
_____
_____
_____
_____
_____
_____
_____
_____
_____
_____
_____
_____
_____
_____

Tip 71: "Create Lesson Plans."

Even if you are not a teacher, writing a book that contains lessons worthy of a lesson plan can educate you and your readers. Inside of each chapter, consider writing a challenge or giving your reader lines to write on as they work through the lesson.

_____

_____

_____

_____

_____

_____

_____

_____

_____

_____

_____

_____

_____

_____

_____

_____

_____

_____

Tip 72: "Write to Heal."

As you begin to write any story, even a business book, emotions will come up for you. They are there to show you that you hold some sort of fear inside. If you will set an intention that you are writing to heal anything inside that may be holding you back from your greatness, you will receive the healing and share it with others who read your story.

_____
_____
_____
_____
_____
_____
_____
_____
_____
_____
_____
_____
_____
_____
_____
_____
_____
_____

Tip 73: "Write to change memories."

Just as you write to heal, you can write to change memories. In the movie *Eat, Pray, Love*, Liz has a time when she remembers her wedding. In her writing, she goes into the memory and changes that memory in her story. Try it.

Tip 74: "Journal in the Middle."

When writing your memoir and if it is based on your journal, take a picture of your actual journal entries and add them to the middle of your book. This JIM method allows you to preserve the marks, strikeouts and emotions of your intimate journal experience and share these experiences with your readers.

_____
_____
_____
_____
_____
_____
_____
_____
_____
_____
_____
_____
_____
_____
_____
_____
_____
_____
_____
_____

Chapter 7 -
It's All About Reaching Out
Marketing made easy tips to reach your ideal
readers and turn them into loyal following!

"Write what should not be forgotten."
— Isabel Allende

Marketing your book can seem like a daunting endeavor. Writing your book is only 10%. Marketing your book is the other 90%.

You are the author so you are the most knowledgeable and invested spokesperson for your book. This portion of you writing journey is yours – yours to direct the path to making your book known.

I highly recommend a strategic marketing plan. However, there are many easy marketing tactics that you can apply immediately to get you, your book, your business, and your brand known.

Sometimes we just need a little guidance to get things going. Here are some "easy to implement" tips you can use to get the word out about your book and be sure that your brand is communicating well with your target reader audience. When you follow these steps, you will be on your way to engaging your audience and seeing progress in your achieving your goals!

Now, discover these top writers' tips, capture your creative thoughts and share your unique story with the world!

Tip 75: "Market like a boss."

Take a look at the new authors on the scene who have created successful marketing campaigns and create a unique message to get your book exposed and popular even before you launch. What are some ways you can comprise a successful marketing strategy?

_____
_____
_____
_____
_____
_____
_____
_____
_____
_____
_____
_____
_____
_____
_____
_____
_____
_____

Tip 76: "Write to speak."

Probably the most important tip in this series is this: Write your book while you plan your speaking career. Every book can and should be a speaking tour. When you write your book, write your speech. Imagine yourself on stage with every person in the audience holding your book. What is your signature speech topic?

_____

_____

_____

_____

_____

_____

_____

_____

_____

_____

_____

_____

_____

_____

_____

_____

_____

Tip 77: "Reflect on the positive."

If you suffer from doubt in your ability, take every moment you can to reflect on the positive aspects of your writing. Even if you have no experience in writing, there is so much positive in you. Note some positive reflections you can include in your marketing here.

_____

_____

_____

_____

_____

_____

_____

_____

_____

_____

_____

_____

_____

_____

_____

_____

_____

_____

Tip 78: "A walk in my shoes lesson."

What is it like to take a walk in your shoes? Teaching your readers to feel empathy is a good skill to have and maintain. Each time they feel they are walking in your shoes, they are diving into your book with wonder and amazement. How can readers take a walk with you?

_____

_____

_____

_____

_____

_____

_____

_____

_____

_____

_____

_____

_____

_____

_____

_____

_____

_____

_____

Tip 79: "Join a Writer's Group."

Locally, there are probably guilds and writing camps, but online there are thousands of writing groups. Find the ones you like and get into the cross-critique conversation. Allow positive and negative feedback to help guide you to present to the world the best possible finished product.

_____

_____

_____

_____

_____

_____

_____

_____

_____

_____

_____

_____

_____

_____

_____

_____

_____

_____

Tip 80: "Create a Sacred Space."

In your home, around your land, even on vacation, create a sacred writing space. Many people love to take their notebook and get under an umbrella on the beach; some enjoy writing by a babbling brook while others like to record their voice while driving. Each time you carve out that sacred space for writing, you are telling the Universe that you are serious about bringing to market your very best.

_____

_____

_____

_____

_____

_____

_____

_____

_____

_____

_____

_____

_____

_____

_____

_____

_____

Tip 81: "Start Your own topic blog."

Having a blog can mean having a book, but keep on topic. If you write about self-improvement and cookie recipes on the same blog, you may end up in mass confusion. Start a topic blog and divide it into 10 sub-topics. Expand each topic and subtopic as deep, wide and unique as possible.

_____
_____
_____
_____
_____
_____
_____
_____
_____
_____
_____
_____
_____
_____
_____
_____
_____
_____
_____

Tip 82: "Guest blog for others."

Being a guest blogger has many amazing benefits, including reaching into someone's list via your contribution to their success. Many companies offer guest bloggers serious promotional opportunities where you can exhibit your book, brand and expand your platform.

_____
_____
_____
_____
_____
_____
_____
_____
_____
_____
_____
_____
_____
_____
_____
_____
_____
_____

Tip 83: "Start a podcast."

Starting a podcast can help you come up with tons of brilliant and fresh ideas. Podcasts are audio recordings that run through a newsfeed and are enjoyed by those who like audio learning. When you host your own podcast, you can interview others, including other writers who you follow and support.

_____
_____
_____
_____
_____
_____
_____
_____
_____
_____
_____
_____
_____
_____
_____
_____
_____
_____

Tip 84: "Tweet with impact."

Twitter, as you know, has become a very popular social media outlet for short posts. When you are forced to write short posts, you must use the greatest impact you can pull from your gut. Make your tweets so delicious that they are clicked every time. Social media is free marketing!

_____

_____

_____

_____

_____

_____

_____

_____

_____

_____

_____

_____

_____

_____

_____

_____

_____

_____

_____

Chapter 8 -
It's All About Your Book
Make your bestseller book the foundation
for your success!

*"Story-tellers and poets spend their lives learning
that skill and art of using words well.
And their words make the souls of their readers
stronger, brighter, deeper."*
— Ursula K. Le Guin

Have you ever dreamed of becoming a bestseller? This title gives you a stamp of credibility that sticks with you forever.

I believe strongly in Amazon Bestsellers for most authors. They are the largest book distributor in the world and determine bestsellers hourly. Programs to assist you with bestseller status can be as low as $2,900.

New York Times, Wall Street Journal and *USA Today* are more subjective in their Bestseller selections and promotions can run $25K - $250K.

In promoting over 1,000 authors to bestseller, I have found that Amazon Bestseller Authors still find their place on major media broadcast, in global publications and their lifetime title brings them enormous benefits in their business/career goals.

Now, discover these top writers' tips, capture your creative thoughts and share your unique story with the world!

Tip 85: "Bestseller status is a tremendous achievement and using this new title can open doors."

When you have a book that has reached the bestseller list, you have shown the world that your book is worthy. Being on this list can be easy or difficult; this choice is yours. Think of this as you are writing and assume within yourself that you are already there.

_____
_____
_____
_____
_____
_____
_____
_____
_____
_____
_____
_____
_____
_____
_____
_____

Tip 86: "How to use your best-selling book to promote yourself in business."

Everyone has a book today. Some say a book is the new business card. When you have a best-selling book, your status quo changes so be on the lookout for ways to show the world who you are through the pages of your book. Find a local company or book store that will allow you to do a book-signing at their location and cross-promote them in all you do. This is a great tool for authors.

_____

_____

_____

_____

_____

_____

_____

_____

_____

_____

_____

_____

_____

_____

_____

Tip 87: "Think Big."

Even self-published authors through CreateSpace or Kindle can sometimes become *New York Times* Best-Selling Authors so "Think Big". See yourself as an author whose books sell over a million copies. What if you sold 1 million copies of your book? How would your life change if your book sold 1 million copies?

_____

_____

_____

_____

_____

_____

_____

_____

_____

_____

_____

_____

_____

_____

_____

_____

_____

_____

_____

Tip 88: "Visualize Success."

Oprah and Ellen both used Vision Boards as part of their success strategy. Visioning is the most powerful self-help tool for anyone, especially authors and writers. When you are building a project, get a poster board, some markers, glue and glitter. Cut out pictures and phrases from magazines and glue them onto your board. Start to vision the success of your work.

_____

_____

_____

_____

_____

_____

_____

_____

_____

_____

_____

_____

_____

_____

_____

_____

Tip 89: "Learn a New Language."

Of course, you want your writing to go global, right? What better way to learn how to succeed in a different country with your writing than to learn how to speak the language of another country? This expands your value and offers a robust set of possibilities for topics.

_____
_____
_____
_____
_____
_____
_____
_____
_____
_____
_____
_____
_____
_____
_____
_____
_____
_____
_____

Tip 90: "Finding Work as a Writer."

Writing is fun that is for sure. But, writing doesn't buy the groceries or pay the electric bill. To find work as a writer, it's an innovative idea to have a resume and an author one-sheet showing your bestseller credentials. Take a look at the going rate for writers in various areas. Upwork.com is a freelance website where employers hire freelance writers for projects such as copywriting and blog creation.

Tip 91: "Fill in the gaps."

There may be areas that you do not have experience, knowledge or the desire to learn to do it yourself. There is a wealth of knowledge free on the web and services offered by tremendous talent, happy to fill in the gaps. Where are your gaps that need to be delegated?

_____

_____

_____

_____

_____

_____

_____

_____

_____

_____

_____

_____

_____

_____

_____

_____

_____

_____

Tip 92: "Become irresistible to the media."

Be sure your press kit is an updated collection of written and online materials designed to introduce you as an expert and your bestseller book to the media. Respond to media inquiries immediately and never turn down an interview!

_____

_____

_____

_____

_____

_____

_____

_____

_____

_____

_____

_____

_____

_____

_____

_____

_____

_____

Tip 93: "Update your website and social media profiles."

Be sure your bestseller status is updated everywhere on the web and in print. Develop or enhance your presence on at a minimum Facebook, Twitter, YouTube and LinkedIn to soar Goggle Ratings for you and your book. Update your website so it is modern and mobile friendly.

Tip 94: "Why self-publish?"

Traditional publishing can take over 18 months if you are accepted and usually requires an agent and they do no marketing for your book. They also take the bulk of your royalties. Self-publishing gives you total control of your book and you can publish as fast as you can write. All royalties come directly to you from the distributor.

_____
_____
_____
_____
_____
_____
_____
_____
_____
_____
_____
_____
_____
_____
_____
_____
_____
_____

Chapter 9 -
It's All About Your Platform

Repurpose your writing to become the foundation
and expansion of your offerings!

"Writing is perhaps the greatest of human inventions, binding together people who never knew each other, citizens of distant epochs. Books break the shackles of time. A book is proof that humans are capable of working magic."
— Carl Sagan

Your Platform is the way that readers, fans and following can participate in your book and your business. It can be set up over time.

It is a funnel they can enter at varying price ranges. The general rule is the more they get of you, the higher the investment.

Perhaps readers can get to know you through a free chapter from your book downloaded online–$0

They then may graduate to buying your book–$+
They are then offered a self-study online class–$++
Perhaps you host a live event–$+++
They join your VIP Day or Mastermind–$++++
Maybe you lead an online class series–$+++++
They are privately mentored by you–$+++++++++

Your book is a perfect foundation for your Platform!

Now, discover these top writers' tips, capture your creative thoughts and share your unique story with the world!

Tip 95: "Know your Platform."

In considering new authors for publishing contracts, traditional publishers want new authors to have a platform or following. As you are writing your book, simultaneously attract your following. Social media is a great place to start.

_____

_____

_____

_____

_____

_____

_____

_____

_____

_____

_____

_____

_____

_____

_____

_____

_____

_____

Tip 96: "Increase your list size through joint ventures."

A joint venture is partnering with another for a book or product launch or on-going referrals and cross-referrals. Once you have a list of 1,000 followers or more, you can start partnering on referrals to increase your list.

_____
_____
_____
_____
_____
_____
_____
_____
_____
_____
_____
_____
_____
_____
_____
_____
_____
_____
_____

Tip 97: "Trade an irresistible gift for visitors to register on your website."

When visitors come to your website, be sure you have an irresistible gift they can register for with their name and email for your list. That gift just could be a chapter of your book. When they redeem their free gift, be sure they can buy your full book on that page. Jot down "to dos" to get your list growing.

_____
_____
_____
_____
_____
_____
_____
_____
_____
_____
_____
_____
_____
_____
_____
_____
_____
_____

Tip 98: "Visit, speak and promote to churches, schools and organizations."

Prearrange approval to take preorders for your book during regular meetings and gatherings, and donate a portion to your favorite charity or organization. You can also take pre-orders on your website and accept payments through a shopping cart or PayPal. Build that list!

Tip 99: "Repurpose your book."

Repurposing is taking the content from your book and using it to create a number of different products. Repurpose your book to create at least 2-3 levels of offerings to your following. Always use a call to action to help them form the habit of doing something after reading your announcements and promotions and purchase your book and products. What will they be?

_____
_____
_____
_____
_____
_____
_____
_____
_____
_____
_____
_____
_____
_____
_____

Tip 100: "Always celebrate your successes."

Celebrate the fact that you are writing. Your writing helps others. Celebrating yourself is the #1 way to feel confident and empowers you to continue writing. I celebrate you!

_____

_____

_____

_____

_____

_____

_____

_____

_____

_____

_____

_____

_____

_____

_____

_____

_____

_____

_____

_____

Chapter 10 -
It's All About the World

Expand Your influence across the globe
and make a difference!

"Writing and reading decrease our sense of isolation. They deepen and widen and expand our sense of life: they feed the soul."
— Anne Lamott

Books should never be treated as items that are only used to look for the information that you need.

Simple as they may be, the book itself can contribute to an individual or a larger group in many different ways, either directly or indirectly. Our seemingly simple action of authoring a book can make a huge difference in our world.

As authors continue to contribute their unique ideas and write books, they are also able to invoke changes to the world by invoking changes in the individual.

A book's influence on a person's knowledge and thinking ability, as a source of inspiration, a means of communication, and how it can start the changes in a person's lifestyle are awesome, and should never be taken for granted.

And, its influence on these global concepts all started in a single person's desire and effort to change the world, and write a book.

Keep writing! *Viki*

About the Author

Viki Winterton is founder of Expert Insights Publishing, home of best-selling and award-winning books and magazines, where visionaries and those on the rise come together to create immediate impact.

Expert Insights Publishing is built on the solid foundation of over 30 years of expertise in promotion, publishing, product development, networking, and success. Fortune 100 companies and individuals across the globe know Viki for fostering powerful and loyal relationships and supporting her communities in wildly creative, unique, and wonderful ways.

Viki is also a multiple #1 international best-selling author and award-winning publisher, international speaker and media magnet, founder of Bestselling Authors International Organization, Write Now! Broadcast and Write Away, Write Now! – the global community where writers find everything they need at each stage of their journey. Viki's publishing company has taken over 1,000 authors to bestseller.

WILL YOU BE NEXT?
ExpertInsightsPublishing.com

Viki's Companies:

The Agency
Bestseller Launchpad
Bestselling Authors International Organization
Beyond Your Book Academy
Founder of Expert Insights Family of Opportunity:
Write Now and Expert Insights Radio
The Coach Exchange Global Community
Bestseller Launchpad Web TV Broadcast
Write Away, Write Now! Learning Center
Expert Insights Publishing Bestseller Books
The Extravaganza and EIPPY Book Awards Events

Viki's #1 International Best-Selling Books:
101 Top Tips for Writers
Are YOU the Missing Piece?
Are YOU the Missing Piece? Workbook
Beyond Your Book
Cancer: From Tears to Triumph
Get Known Workbook
My Big Idea Book
My Big Idea Workbook
My Creative Thoughts Journal
My Creative Thoughts Workbook
PR Magnet
Ready, Aim, Captivate!
Ready, Aim, Excel!
Ready, Aim, Impact!
Ready, Aim, Influence!
Ready, Aim, Inspire!
Ready, Aim, Soar!
Ready, Aim, Thrive!
Tail Waggin' Tales
Wounded? Survive! Thrive!!!

Viki's Award-Winning Magazines:
Insights
PUBLISHED!
Stress Free
Resources Uncovered

Viki's Award-Winning Videos:
https://www.youtube.com/playlist?list=PL5u0HomaU
TodmBLJzBVE3DY6bIFXTkT9R

Resources

**Become a Best-Selling Author and
Radio PR Magnet Comprehensive Class**
BookRadio.Expert

Bestseller Launchpad
bestsellerlaunchpad.com

Bestselling Authors International Organization
bestsellingauthorsinternational.org

Beyond Your Book Academy
beyondyourbookacademy.com

Extravaganza and EIPPY Book Awards
MyBookAward.com

Get Known Now!
expertinsightspublishing.com/HowtoGetKnownNow.
html

***PUBLISHED!* Magazine**
expertinsightspublishing.com/PUBLISHEDGift.html

Write Away, Write Now Global Community
writeawaywritenow.com

Expert Insights Radio
http://www.blogtalkradio.com/writenow

Write Now! Radio
http://www.blogtalkradio.com/expertsinsights